The DEBT DIET

MARQUIS BOOKER

outskirts
press™

CONTENTS

INTRODUCTION

THE AVERAGE PERSON LOOKS at saving money as a huge mountain to climb. They tend to look at all the bills, all the financial responsibilities, and all the obstacles that come with money. The car note, the groceries, the day care, the credit cards, the utilities, and that one monster we all must face, the mortgage/rent. This is a scary thought or feeling when you think about all this, then try to figure out how do I even begin to think about saving money? No way! How can I begin to think about paying off debt? No way! Well, you've picked up this book so you're already thinking about it, and you've already taken a step, one step, towards your "*Debt Diet,*"and I'm here to help.

Within this book I will try to lay out steps that I used to get back on track, build credit, reduce and/or eliminate debt, and build savings and investments. I know the "build investments" part sounds scary but don't worry, this is a reference for you to get there in your own time, in your own way, and on your own scale. So now that we have talked about all the things that stress you out and prohibit you from even beginning to get your path started—all those bills, all the anxiety about how to start, and the scary words like investment and debt—I need you to do ONE thing. Forget about all that!!!

The *"Debt Diet"* is no different from any other regular diet. When you begin a diet you think about what parts of your body you want to work on. For most of us it's that stubborn belly fat, I'm just saying. Then you tend to think of what you need to do to get rid of it, be it some form of cardio or exercise in general. Next, you may start to think about what to eat to achieve that goal. When you work with a meal planner, they may ask you what type of foods you like, so they can create a plan specific for you to achieve your goal. They may give you a certain weight to hit by a certain time or a certain number of calories you need to target to achieve your goal. It's the same thing with money. You must start with a plan and break that into smaller pieces. Don't be overwhelmed by everything at once. You don't just hit the gym and max out the weight, you start with a lighter weight and work your way up. When you start your meal plan you typically start by replacing a few items at a time, you don't just go all veggies the next day—that typically never works. Just like any meal, you take a lot of small bites to complete it. You must do the same with money goals: take one small bite at a time.

Here are a couple of small bites you can start with.......

Chapter 1
"THE WARMUP"

HOW DO I START? You can't figure out the solution to anything in life if you don't know the problem, right? When you decide you need to go on a diet it is usually because you've identified some physical attribute about yourself you are not happy with. You may step on a scale and see how much you weigh. You may look in a mirror and not like a certain part of your body. You may even take pictures to know where you will be able to see the results later. Same with money. Let's identify where we are first to figure out our next step to get to where we want to be. Notice I said figure out where we are to figure out *our next step*, not figure out where we are to get to where we want to be. I believe this is where most people make the mistake. If you look so far ahead, you tend to get discouraged. We are going to take small steps, small bites. Our only goal is the next step. One bite at a time, remember?

So, let's look at our weight on the scale or that image in the mirror, so to speak. How much money do I bring home per month? Don't look at the year, just each month on average. I said "bring home." This is the money you have left after Uncle Sam takes his cut, the insurance and 401k deductions, and any other things that are coming out before you see that final number on your check or in your bank account. This is called your NET income. Be honest with yourself—don't include side jobs you don't work all year or bonuses you may or may not receive. Keep it simple. Write that number down. Put it in a spreadsheet if you want to be fancy, or whatever way you want to track this. The main goal is to know this number. You must know what you bring in to begin to solve the problem, and this will be the foundation your journey will be built on. You can't go to a trainer and tell him you weigh 160 pounds when you know you weigh 190 pounds. You can't get to where you are going if you are not honest about where you are. Is it too early in the book to go there, too deep? OK, stay with me. We are in this together.

Now that we have established what we bring home

monthly after taxes, insurance, and other deductions, which we now know is called "net" income, let's look at where it's going. Yeah, it's time to get down to the ugly truth. You remember when you thought to yourself that you just don't make enough to save, or you just have too many bills to save? I'm pretty sure that after this step you will be surprised. Now that we know how many calories we take in per month, or net income, let's see how many calories we burn monthly, or how much we spend.

In this step you don't necessarily have to separate what you are spending by category but feel free to do so if you want. At this point we just want to get the overall dollar amount you spend monthly or what we call "expenditures." You can use your bank statement or just scroll down that bank app on your phone and write it down and add it up. This will tell us how many calories we burn monthly, i.e., how much we spend. Now that you have both numbers, subtract the amount you spend from the amount you make. What is the difference? I'm willing to bet you have something left over, even if it's your last two dollars. Am I right or am I right? It's not magic—you just can't spend what you don't have. Well, some of us do when we run those credit cards up that we can't pay off, but we will get to that later. I'm not here to judge. I did it too. Don't get mad at me just yet. Remember, we are in this together.

Now that we know what we bring home (our net income), what we spend (our expenditures), and the difference between the two, this is where we start. Take the last two dollars you had in your account and SAVE IT! Make sure you put it in a high-interest savings account that is not tied to your checking, preferably at a different bank from your checking account. Make sure you sign up for paperless statements. "Out of sight, out of mind." Do not get an ATM card for this account if offered. Do not sign up to the online app. You want zero access to this account unless you physically walk into a bank or credit union during business hours and make a withdrawal, which we are not planning to do any time soon, right? Right! What are you going to do with two dollars anyway? Just kidding.

I know what you are thinking. You're thinking I read this book to go through all that to save two dollars a month?! No. Don't forget, we are taking a small bite to finish a meal. This is only the beginning so hang in there. The last two dollars represent the beginning of you creating a habit of saving. I promise you when you get to the end of the month you will try to go from two dollars to an even five dollars. I suppose five is not even, but you get the picture. You will start to pay more attention to what is left when you get to the 26th, 27th, or 28th day of the month.

Remember when we talked about being

discouraged? People tend to think saving money must be done one hundred, two hundred, or a thousand dollars at a time. When they can't hit that expectation, they tend to just spend what's left and give up until the next time they get that bonus or income tax refund. The only expectation in this step is to save something no matter how small. Besides, I'm going to show you how to grow those last two dollars later in the book. Relax, grab a glass of wine, and continue reading. By the way, if you did grab that wine, you could have put that money you spent on that bottle with those two dollars and saved a little bit more. See, I'm showing you how to grow it already.

Chapter 11
"THE MEAL PREP"

NOW THAT WE KNOW what we make and what we spend, and at the end of the month we move that last two dollars, or whatever that number is, from our checking account to a high-interest savings account at a different bank with a paperless account and no ATM card, what do we do next? What is the next step? The next bite? Well, I'm glad you asked.

Remember that list of expenditures you made in Chapter I? Let's go back and take a closer look. Remember, expenditures are the things you spent money on. I'm sure as you are going back through this you have noticed a lot of little and most likely unnecessary things you've spent money on. Things that you didn't really need, or you could cut back on if you are honest with yourself. Don't act like you didn't see the coffee you buy every other day or all the fast food that you eat half of and stick the rest in the fridge until it goes bad. No, not you? Is it the shoes or clothes that you saw? How about brunch? Still not you? Maybe it's the subscriptions you pay for and are not using that you forgot about? Yeah, you saw something. Don't worry, I'm not here to tell you to give all that up. We're taking small bites, remember. I know it's hard to go cold turkey so I'm not going to ask you to. As I said before, that rarely works. What I do want you to do is identify the one item you probably could cut back on just a little bit if you had to. I'll give you a minute. You could just stop reading this book and take longer than a minute to think about it, but you shouldn't have to, because you already know what that one thing is. You knew as soon as I said it.

Now that you have your item, I want you to cut out two purchases a month, that's it. If that item was coffee and it cost you five dollars for every purchase, then you commit to save the price of two coffees per month and save ten dollars per month. Also, you could just drink cheaper coffee every now and then, I'm just saying. However, if you want to do it, just choose to save the cost of that purchase, whatever it is. That sounds simple enough, right? Afterall, this was an item you said you could do without if you really had to. I can't let you get off that easy though. People tend to spend money they can see and have instant access to. So, I want you to save those ten dollars, or whatever your number is in advance. Start a direct deposit of ten dollars into that high-interest savings account we opened in Chapter I. You remember, the paperless one that we don't have an ATM card for.

Look at that! We haven't even gotten into the meat and potatoes of this diet yet and we've already saved $144 per year at least, and you thought you couldn't do it. Don't forget that additional one to two percent interest you are making in that high-interest savings account that is paperless and we have no ATM card for. I think you get the point by now. Just needed to say it again for those of you who may get or may have gotten the ATM card just in case. Take the temptation out of your way. We don't go on a diet and go buy a steak and put it in the fridge "just in case" the diet doesn't work. Follow the process. You deserve it. Your kids deserve it. Your family deserves it.

Now I've given some guidelines and ideas here but feel free to give up three cups of coffee or whatever your item or items may be. The point of this step or, as we call it, this bite, is to do something that you can sustain. One bite at a time. Like a regular diet, people tend to give up when they go all in on Day One. This is still a small step. Our goal here is to create a habit of saving. As you continue and saving becomes second nature you will start to get excited about the possibilities. Similar to losing weight, it is so much of a struggle to work out and eat right. Then when you notice your pants are starting to feel too big, you get excited about the progress. It's the same with money.

Chapter III

"THE PRE-WORKOUT BOOST"

NOW THAT WE KNOW what we make, what we spend, have cut two cups of coffee per month, and saved another two dollars per month at each month's end, we now have a total of about $144 per year in a high-interest savings account with...............well, you know where I'm going with this.

I'm sure you are thinking you spent the last two chapters doing all that work just to save $144 a year, but you would be wrong. If you haven't gotten it by now, you spent the time reading those chapters to create a habit, a routine, a simple process. Nothing happens by chance when it comes to saving. Every successful person started with a plan to reach their goals. Once they put a plan in place, they follow the steps within that plan to get there and stay there. You must do the same with money. You can't depend on a big influx of cash like an income tax refund to get started. If you don't start before that tax money hits your account, chances are you won't start after it does.

At this point in your journey, I would advise you to go back through the first two chapters and see how you can comfortably increase your savings. Maybe for you it's giving up two cups of coffee and that bag of chips and soda you buy from the store on your way home when you are just supposed to be getting gas. Maybe it's finding a savings account with a higher return. Maybe it's making sure that two dollars at the end of each month is six or eight dollars, if not every month, then every other month. The important thing is making sure you are comfortable with whatever your number is. Remember, these are small bites. The goal is to just start.

Check this out! This next step towards freedom does not call for you to give up anything. Yeah, no joke, you really don't have to give up anything in this step—well, nothing you buy every month anyway. I want to remind you how important it is at this point not to check your balance on that savings account. This boost that we are about to talk about will definitely make you want to take a peek, especially if you are a couple months into your journey and have maximized the process from the first two chapters. Pinky promise you won't look? OK, well, promise you won't look again any time soon.

It's time we put a little fire on that savings account to get our juices flowing and get us a little excited. Although this step is in Chapter III, I would advise doing this in your first month. The reason I did not mention it until now is that I wanted you to build the habit first. If you are unable to save and have not started, like getting that tax refund, you most likely will be apt to just spend the money you get from this boost rather than save it. Now that you have a plan in place and created a habit, we can add a little boost.

SELL EVERYTHING!

OK, maybe not everything, but what about all that stuff in storage that you don't use and don't need? (I'll get into cutting costs like this later in the book so don't steal my thunder.) What about all those clothes in your closet or children's closet, especially the stuff with the tags still on it, that you all never wear or have grown out of? How about all those toys the kids only played with once or twice? Old dishes, pots, and pans, or the workout equipment in the garage with boxes sitting on them? What about the old car you were supposed to fix up five years ago? Did I go too far? Good! Our goal is to save money, not things.

How important is that stuff to you compared to financial freedom, paying for your kids' college fund, setting yourself up for retirement, or paying off student loans? Is keeping this stuff more important than the stress and anxiety you've been feeling because you're living check to check? Something to think about. After you finish thinking, SELL IT!

Now that you have sold everything and you're standing there with a fist full of cash, I bet you're thinking about how you are going to really stack up that savings account. NOT!

Most likely you are thinking about all the things you "need" to buy. But it's OK. It's normal. I'm not here to make you stress even more about money. I want you to build a habit and not stress about it, so take half of what you've earned and go crazy. Buy the things you want because we both know those were "wants" and not "needs" you were thinking about a few lines back. Take the other half and go deposit it as soon as possible. Remember, you made a pinky promise that you wouldn't peek at the balance.

Chapter IV

"THE WORKOUT"

BY NOW, WE KNOW what we make, we know what we spend, we've started making saving a habit, and we've given our account a little boost. We can move into the main workout.

You might be saying at this point, OK, this book is giving me a little something to work with. Hopefully, by the time you get to this chapter, you have started consistently saving. Yes, I know some people read the entire book sometimes before even starting but I'm hoping you'll continue to use this handbook as a reference. If that's the case, go back through the first few chapters again and see how you can pour gas on what you've already been doing. Did you kick that coffee habit yet? No? What about that workout equipment with the dust on it in the garage? No? That's OK. I'm not here to judge.

Well, we've come this far so let's dig in a little deeper. As you can see by now, this book is not talking about budgets, investing, 401ks, and IRAs—all the big words that typically confuse people and scare them away from finance. Although all this is very important, we are here to start small, be comfortable, create good savings habits, and maximize those habits. Once we have mastered these habits, we can move into some of those big words in my next book, if anyone reads this one. But you're reading it right now, so I guess I'm off to a good start. Besides, if I can help one person get started on the right track that would be amazing. Tell you what, I'll at least break down some of those big words at the end so you will have a simple understanding of them later in the book.

This part of the journey is the big boy/big girl portion. We're into the "meat and potatoes" now. We need to get on the phone with our creditors and make threats. No, not those types of threats. We need to ask for better rates, lower payments, discounts, deals, fees to be waived, or whatever they have to offer us. All they can say is no and if they do, then no harm, no foul. But most times if you let them know you plan on leaving, closing that card, changing your provider, or whatever leverage you have as a good customer, they typically will get you to an account manager to offer you something to keep you as a customer. If not, then ask to speak to their boss. You may need to be aggressive with some, but the result will be worth it. Go for the gold. The worst thing that can happen is your bill stays the same. Call your credit card lenders and ask if they can offer a better rate, waive some yearly and or monthly fees if you happen to have no balance, and call the cable company and ask if they have any promotions available you can take advantage of. Let them know you are thinking about canceling the service. Call your cell phone provider, light company, everybody. I think you will be surprised at what you can achieve.

This part of the journey gets more aggressive. At this point, I would hope you are four to six months into it, so you have built up a tolerance for saving. If not, it's OK. Feel free to make these calls on Day One if you'd like. The reason I chose to wait until this far into the book, other than wanting you to form a habit and build tolerance for saving, is that I want every dime you save from making these calls to go into your savings account monthly. That's a long way from those two dollars we started with, right? You are probably thinking, "You want me to just put all this money I saved into a savings account?" Hey, you were just giving it away a couple of hours ago before you made those calls. May as well give it to yourself. Not the guys from the first couple of chapters, right? OK, how about 40 percent of what you save goes into saving monthly, Is that better? But don't short yourself, work towards 100 percent. You deserve it.

Chapter V

"THE PROTEIN SHAKE"

NOW THAT WE HAVE learned all the things we can do to reduce our debt on what we call the "Debt Diet," what's next? Where do we go from here? Of course, the first thing I will say is to go back through the initial steps in this book and see how you can magnify those. What can you add? What more can you do?

At this point, if you have done almost everything you can do to reduce your debt, you may be feeling like you hit a wall and that's OK. I know you are thinking, how can you say it's OK, you're supposed to help us save money. That can't be it, right? Well, unfortunately, there is somewhat of a limit to how much you can realistically save and have some quality of life. You want to save money and still be able to live life with your family, take a vacation, and simply capture memories with your loved ones. Although there is a ceiling to how much you can save off what you currently make, there is no limit to how much more you can make. That's the good news.

Now that you know what to do with money when you get it and you've created a habit of saving, you can throw fuel on the fire by making more money. There is no limit to how much you can make and these days there are a lot of ways to make money. The most popular and common way to do this is to trade time for money. You give a company hours of your time and they pay you to do a task during that time. Yeah, we call it a job. Man, I'm good. Bet you didn't know that. OK, I know you know that but it's important that you look at it through the eyes of trading time for money because if you ever plan to be rich and stay rich you must make money work for you. Just like there's a limit to how much you can save, there is a limit to how many hours you can trade for money. So, where do we start?

Most people are not familiar with those big words we talked about being afraid of, like IRAs, stocks, bonds, etc. This most likely describes some of you reading this book, so the best thing to do is put this on cruise control and start with the professionals. You probably already have a professional on your team that you are not using to their full potential. Start with your 401k at your job. If you are not familiar with the investment world, then sit back and let the professionals do it for you. A 401k is simply a retirement savings plan. Don't get scared by the name. The 401k name simply comes from the section of the tax code that describes it. Too complicated? Yeah, I know. It is just a savings plan— let's keep it simple. Most companies offer this and the money comes straight out of your check and goes into this savings plan for you. The great thing about this savings plan is that the money being taken out is tax-free. It goes into your savings plan before Uncle Sam, FICA, or any other name you use for the government takes a piece.

The other great thing about a 401k or as we call it, a savings plan, is that most employers match up to a certain percentage of what you put in. Wow, do you understand what type of fuel you just added to the fire? If you put in 3 percent of your income and your company matches that 3 percent you've just made a 100 percent return on your money without doing a thing. You doubled your money! Isn't that exciting? Some may only match 100 percent on 1 percent and then 50 percent on anything up to a certain percentage.

It's structured in many ways. Either way, it's additional money going into your savings plan. Ask your benefits department what that match is.

In some cases, companies may allow you to put in or contribute more than they will match. I would say put in as much as they allow on the high end. At a minimum, I suggest putting in as much as they will match. Where else can you go and get a 100 percent return on your money? Confused yet? Listen, the key here is to find out what percentage your company matches and contribute that to your 401k. For those of you stock-market-savvy folks, we do understand the market goes up and down so the 100 percent return on your money part is not digging into all that. The goal is to tell those who don't know, that if they contribute a buck and their company contributes a buck, they will double what they contribute.

Outside of that high-interest savings account we've talked about throughout this book, this is a great protein shake to add to your workout and fuel your net worth without trading additional time for money.

The money in your 401k is being invested for you by the company that holds it, such as Vanguard, which is a popular one that a lot of companies partner with. Most times they invest based on some basic questions you answered when you set it up, such as the year you plan to retire, whether you want to invest aggressively, and things like that. Most people will set this up and forget about it and never investigate what they set up. That can still work, but you do have options available. You can pay a small fee to have someone actively manage your account, which means a real person or people will look at your account, usually on a yearly basis, and move your money around based on what's going on with the economy and/or the stock market in hopes to get higher returns for you. You can also pay a smaller fee and have your investment account robot-managed, which means exactly what it sounds like. A robot/machine will evaluate and move money accordingly. These fees can be worth your while and make a huge impact on your account over the span of 10, 20, or 30 years. Talk to the professionals. Ask them which has worked best over the last few years and see what works for you. Traditional IRAs and Roth IRAs are also great ways to move into the next level of having your money work for you, but I won't get into that in this book as we are talking about creating habits and keeping it simple this round. Maybe we can break those down in that next book I talked about.

So, you may be thinking, dude, the title of this book is "The Debt Diet" and all you have talked about is saving money, IRAs, and 401ks. Well, you can't get out of debt without the tools and money to do it. Everything you've learned and/or have been reminded of to this point are those small bites that provide the fuel to get to the end goal: GET OUT OF DEBT! You can't get out of debt without the money to do so. More important is forming the habit of continuing to make money and having your money make money to help you do so. Am I bringing it all home for you now?

Now, some people say you should pay off the debts with the highest interest rate. Some say take the smallest debt first. I say pick one and pay one. Doesn't matter. Pick the one that feels right for you. The most important thing is to pay something off. Which one will get you the most excited to get rid of? For me, paying off something like a dishwasher I got on credit is the one I want to see gone. It would kill me to pay a couple hundred dollars a month on something that brings me no joy. Now a big-screen TV, on the other hand, I wouldn't mind as much. Of course, that would be something I got before I read this book. All jokes aside, just pay something off or pick one and start aggressively paying it off, then move to the next. Grow and repeat the steps in this book until you do. You will be out of debt before you know it.

Chapter VI

"THE COOL DOWN"

NOW THAT WE ARE professional debt dieters, you are ready to roll. Well, maybe we got everything to this point except that 401k stuff—that was a lot, right? LOL. Keep referring to that chapter and make sure you call your provider and ask questions. It's your money and they are there to help. All you have to do is call.

So, think about why you are reading this book. What made you pick it up or order it? What made you seek out ways to save money? For most of us the root cause would be that we were never taught anything about money by our parents. Is that you? Maybe we learned about it after we began having issues when we were older in life, and we are trying to correct that at this point. Maybe we knew a little something and we are trying to put fuel on that fire. Maybe we're young and want to start out on the right foot. Whatever the reason, now that you've got it, I challenge you to pass it on to your family. Especially your kids.

Teach some people around you about some basic things you've done on your journey as early as possible to start creating that savings habit. Finance can be scary, but learning one or two tips about something as simple as saving from someone you know is less invasive. The earlier they start, the better off they will be. I challenge you to change ONE life. Remember this book was written as a simple handbook with a few ideas to help you take one step in the right direction. Although I gave you some action plans that I've done, there are many more you can do. Your way may work better for you. Only you know your situation and your tendencies and what will sit right with you and your lifestyle. This is definitely not the end-all be-all to get to your end goal. Think outside the box, then share your truth with the ones you love.

The last part I want you to consider is not only making sure you set your beneficiary on those accounts you have, but also getting a will drawn up. Yes, a will. You can never be too young to draw up a will. Contrary to popular belief this is not something you need to wait until you are older to do. If you are reading this book you are old enough to draw up a will or living trust. If you have a spouse or children, you need it. Take some of that money you saved and do that now. **It's very important to protect what you've built. It's more important that we build up those we protect!** Man, that was good. Just came to me out of nowhere. No way I can top that, so I'll end my thoughts here. Be Blessed and Good Luck!